TUDOR
1485–1603

STUART
1603–1714

GEORGIAN
1714–1837

children's HISTORY of
LINCOLNSHIRE

Written by
Neil Tonge

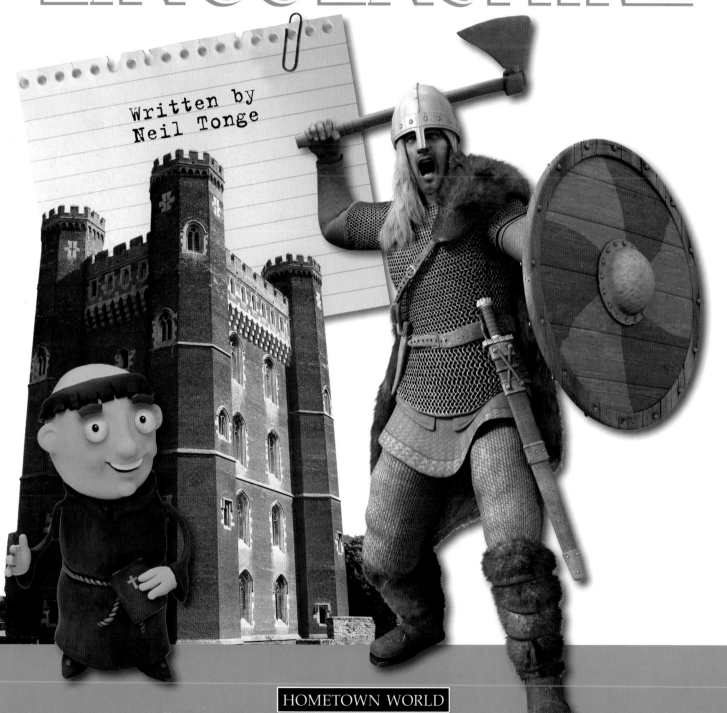

HOMETOWN WORLD

How well do you know Lincolnshire?

Have you ever wondered what it would have been like living in Lincolnshire when the Vikings arrived? What about when the first ever railways were built? This book will uncover the important and exciting things that happened in this wonderful county.

Some rather brainy folk have worked on this book to make sure it's fun and informative. So what are you waiting for? Peel back the pages and be amazed at Lincolnshire's very own story.

Timeline shows which period (dates and people) each spread is talking about

'Spot this!' game with something to find in the county

THE FACTS

The Romans are Coming

The Romans are marching north towards Lincolnshire. Should we fight them or try to make a treaty of friendship? Many of the young warriors want to attack.

"Fight, fight! Are we not proud Celts?" shouts Druca, their leader.

My father, chieftain of the tribe, tries to calm him. "We are too few and the Romans are too strong. It is best we choose the path of peace."

His wise words win the day.

Who were the Romans?

The Romans invaded Britain in AD 43. They came from Italy, and had built up a huge empire which covered most of Europe. Their next step was to cross the English Channel. Why did they come to Britain? There was a new Roman emperor, called Claudius, who wanted to show he was a bold and warlike leader. He also wanted Britain's riches, such as grain, tin, iron and gold.

The powerful Roman army landed in south-east England. Very quickly, it took control of the area where London now stands. From here, smaller forces set out to the west and the north to conquer more land.

By about AD 100, the Romans ruled most of the south, east and west of Britain. But they never conquered the far north of England or Scotland, or took control of Wales. Nor did they try to invade Ireland.

Mosaics are made from hundreds of pieces of coloured stone, like this one at Horkstow Roman Villa.

Rebellion

The Celtic tribe who lived in Lincolnshire, the Corieltauvi (pronounced 'Coreel-tauvee'), were a small clan who decided it was better to be friendly with the Romans than to fight them. A fort was built on the present-day site of Lincoln, which the Romans called Lindum.

In AD 60, a savage revolt broke out, led by Queen Boudicca of the neighbouring Iceni tribe. Many Romans were killed but afterwards a Roman army defeated them and killed Boudicca. To make Britain safer, the Romans decided to move northwards and soon a new frontier was made along Hadrian's Wall in the north of England.

Lindum was no longer needed as a fighting fortress. Retired Roman soldiers were encouraged to settle in Lincoln and the town became what the Romans called a 'colonia'.

A typical Roman Fort

Towns and Roads

The Romans changed the landscape of Britain in many ways. They built towns and forts as centres for governing areas they had conquered. Between these they laid a network of roads, so that soldiers could move quickly from place to place. When Hadrian's Wall was built, it acted as a barrier to keep Roman territory separate from the barbarians on the other side.

FUN FACT
Gold and silver rings found in Lincolnshire show the Celtic god Toutatis, who drowned his victims by plunging them headfirst into a vat of liquid.

SPOT THIS!
The Newport Arch was one of the main gateways into the Roman fort of Lincoln. Can you spot it?

4

... AD 43 ROMANS INVADE BRITAIN.. AD 60 BOUDICCA LEADS REVOLT...

AD 122 HADRIAN'S WALL IS BUILT.. AROUND AD 200 NEWPORT ARCH IS BUILT...   5

Intriguing photos

Fun Facts to amaze you!

THE EVIDENCE

Once the Romans settled, they built large farmhouses called villas. Local Celtic nobleman began to copy the ways of the Romans. In the imaginary account below, a Celtic British boy tells us about life in his new villa.

'Lin' was the Celtic name for a pool. 'Coln' comes from our word 'colonia' – a settlement for retired Roman legionaries.

My Celtic name is Bradan but Father tells me it's better to use my Roman name, Marcus. My father supplies the Roman forts with grain. This has made us very rich. Now Father has plans to make our villa as great as any Roman's.

We already have hot baths and under-floor heating. We also have plenty of slaves to work for us. In fact, I have my own personal slave! He's Greek and is well educated. He's teaching me Latin – the language the Romans speak.

Father has now decided that the best villas have mosaics, so workmen have arrived and are showing him their clever designs. My favourite shows a chariot race. I hope father chooses that one!

Jars like this one were used to store wine, fish sauce and olive oil.

Roman coins like these were coined by the Corieltauvi long before the Roman invasion.

We Romans left Britain in about AD 410 to defend our territories abroad.

How do we know?

In 1797, workers were clearing the ground to make a garden at Horkstow Hall in north Lincolnshire when they accidentally discovered a beautiful Roman mosaic. It is one of the largest ever found in Britain. This has given archaeologists a better understanding of how rich and prosperous the villas were in Roman Lincolnshire.

Other artefacts from the site included Roman coins from the 3rd century, red Roman pottery called Samian ware and quernstones for grinding corn into flour. In 1927, the British Museum took out the remaining fragments and in 1979, Hull Museum put the finds on display.

6   7

An imaginary account of what it was like for children growing up in Lincolnshire

A summary explaining how we know about the past

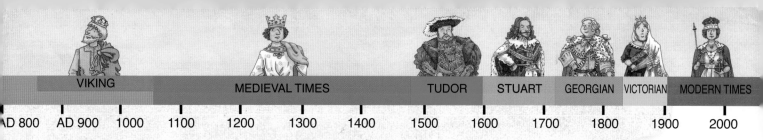

Contents

The Romans are Coming   4

Raiders!   8

Dragons!   12

Rebellion   14

Faith and Fear   16

New Machines   20

Wartime   24

Today and Tomorrow   28

Glossary   30
Index   31
Acknowledgements   32

The Romans are Coming

The Romans are marching north towards Lincolnshire. Should we fight them or try to make a treaty of friendship? Many of the young warriors want to attack.

"Fight, fight! Are we not proud Celts?" shouts Druca, their leader.

My father, chieftain of the tribe, tries to calm him. "We are too few and the Romans are too strong. It is best we choose the path of peace."

His wise words win the day.

Who were the Romans?

The Romans invaded Britain in AD 43. They came from Italy, and had built up a huge empire which covered most of Europe. Their next step was to cross the English Channel. Why did they come to Britain? There was a new Roman emperor, called Claudius, who wanted to show he was a bold and warlike leader. He also wanted Britain's riches, such as grain, tin, iron and gold.

The powerful Roman army landed in south-east England. Very quickly, it took control of the area where London now stands. From here, smaller forces set out to the west and the north to conquer more land.

By about AD 100, the Romans ruled most of the south, east and west of Britain. But they never conquered the far north of England or Scotland, or took control of Wales. Nor did they try to invade Ireland.

Mosaics, like this one at Horkstow Roman villa, are made from hundreds of pieces of coloured stone.

Rebellion

The Celtic tribe who lived in Lincolnshire, the Corieltauvi (pronounced 'Coreel-tauvee'), were a small clan who decided it was better to be friendly with the Romans than to fight them. A fort was built on the present-day site of Lincoln, which the Romans called Lindum.

In AD 60, a savage revolt broke out, led by Queen Boudicca of the neighbouring Iceni tribe. Many Romans were killed, and afterwards a Roman army defeated the Iceni and killed Boudicca. To make Britain safer, the Romans decided to move northwards and soon a new frontier was made along Hadrian's Wall in the north of England.

Lindum was no longer needed as a fighting fortress. Retired Roman soldiers were encouraged to settle in Lincoln and the town became what the Romans called a 'colonia'.

SPOT THIS!

The Newport Arch was one of the main gateways into the Roman fort of Lincoln. Can you spot it?

Towns and Roads

The Romans changed the landscape of Britain in many ways. They built towns and forts as centres for governing areas they had conquered. Between these they laid a network of roads, so that soldiers could move quickly from place to place. When Hadrian's Wall was built, it acted as a barrier to keep Roman territory separate from the barbarians on the other side.

A typical Roman fort

FUN FACT

Gold and silver rings found in Lincolnshire show the Celtic god Toutatis, who drowned his victims by plunging them headfirst into a vat of liquid.

Once the Romans settled, they built large farmhouses called villas. Local Celtic noblemen began to copy the ways of the Romans. In the imaginary account below, a Celtic British boy tells us about life in his new villa.

'Lin' was the Celtic name for a pool. 'Coln' comes from our word 'colonia' – a settlement for retired Roman legionaries.

My Celtic name is Bradan but Father tells me it's better to use my Roman name, Brennus. My father supplies the Roman forts with grain. This has made us very rich. Now Father has plans to make our villa as great as any Roman's.

We already have hot baths and under-floor heating. We also have plenty of slaves to work for us. In fact, I have my own personal slave! He's Greek and is well educated. He's teaching me Latin – the language the Romans speak.

Father has now decided that the best villas have mosaics, so workmen have arrived and are showing him their clever designs. My favourite shows a chariot race. I hope Father chooses that one!

Roman coins like these were copied by the Corieltauvi long before the Roman invasion.

Jars like this one were used to store wine, fish sauce and olive oil.

How do we know?

In 1797, workers were clearing the ground to make a garden at Horkstow Hall in north Lincolnshire when they accidentally discovered a beautiful Roman mosaic. It is one of the largest ever found in Britain. This has given archaeologists a better understanding of how rich and prosperous the villas were in Roman Lincolnshire. In 1927, the British Museum took out the remaining fragments of the mosaic and, in 1979, Hull Museum put them on display in their Roman Gallery.

Other artefacts from the site included Roman coins from the 3rd century, red Roman pottery called Samian ware and quernstones for grinding corn into flour.

We Romans left Britain in about AD 410 to defend our territories abroad.

Raiders!

The Saxons have been raiding the shores ever since the Romans left. A small party of Saxon warriors has landed on the shore but this time there are women and children with them. Some people in Lindsey think it may be possible for everyone to live peaceably together. But others disagree. Before long, a quarrel breaks out and local people begin to fight with the Saxon strangers.

Who were the Anglo-Saxons?

Map of Angle-Land AD 600–900

PICTLAND

Antonine Wall

STRATHCLYDE

Hadrian's Wall

NORTHUMBRIA

LINDSEY

EAST ANGLIA

MERCIA

ESSEX

HWICCA

KENT

WESSEX   SUSSEX

N

The Anglo-Saxons were not a single tribe but a mixture of different peoples from the areas of Europe we now know as Denmark and Germany. Among these were the Angles, the Saxons and the Jutes. All of them had fast-growing populations and were eager to find new land to settle on.

Saxon raiders began attacking the south-east coast of England in about AD 350. After Roman power collapsed in around AD 410, other Anglo-Saxon groups crossed the sea to southern Britain. Within 200 years, they had taken control of all the land up to the borders of Scotland and Wales. It became known as 'Angle-land', or England.

Anglo-Saxon England was divided into Kingdoms. Lincolnshire was then part of Lindsey.

Lindsey

Lindsey – also known as Linnuis – was the Anglo-Saxon kingdom covering roughly the same area as modern-day Lincolnshire, mainly north of the River Witham. We know that the Saxons were already in Lindsey by the end of the 4th century, hired by the Romans to defend the shores of Britain. Sometimes there were quarrels but we know from evidence of place names that many of the British and Saxon communities lived side by side. Towns, however, went into decline after the Romans left and the people of Lindsey were living in small villages.

Lincoln probably remained important, becoming the capital of Lindsey. But Lindsey was sandwiched between two more powerful Saxon kingdoms. To the south lay Mercia and, to the north, Northumbria. By the 9th century, Lindsey had been swallowed up into Mercia.

SPOT THIS!

Part of St Giles Church at Scartho in Grimsby is from Anglo-Saxon times. Can you find out which part?

Most Saxons lived in small huts like this one.

Together, the Angles and Saxons are known as Anglo-Saxons.

FUN FACT

A separate tribe of Angles, the Spaldingas, settled in what is now the area around the town of Spalding.

A Holy Place

The Anglo-Saxons left us a huge legacy: Christianity. The earliest settlers were pagans, which means they worshipped many different nature gods. But from about AD 600, Christian missionaries from Ireland and mainland Europe converted many people. Britain became a Christian country for the first time.

St Paulinus visited Linnuis and converted Blaecca, the chieftain of Lindsey, in AD 629. After this, churches and monasteries spread throughout the kingdom. Meanwhile, Crowland, Bardney and Hibaldstow became important centres of learning.

In this imaginary account, a 10-year-old Saxon girl called Acca tells us about Paulinus's visit to Linnuis in AD 629.

It was a very exciting day. Paulinus is like a celebrity!

What a strange day! We were told that an important man was coming to our town, Linnuis, and that we must all go and greet him. Father kept scolding us to hurry up and finally we set off for the lodge of our king, Blaecca.

After bustling around, a sudden silence fell upon the crowd of people. They parted like a slow moving wave and a tall man walked between them. It was Paulinus! I thought he would have been dressed in fine clothing but instead he was dressed very simply in a long brown woollen robe.

Paulinus climbed upon a large flat stone and told us that God would save us all but we must give up the old gods. There is only one god, he explained, and it is to this god we must pray. Some people in the crowd murmured in disapproval but Blaecca held up his hand and told us that we must obey.

SAXON PLACE NAMES

-ham = village

-tun or -ton = farm

ley- = clearing in woodland

stow- = meeting place

try- = tree

worth- = settlement with a stockade around it

Do you live somewhere that was originally settled by the Saxons?

FUN FACT

Many people believed there was no such kingdom as Lindsey, until archaeologists began to find evidence.

The Anglo-Saxon Chronicle was a record of key events at the time. It was written by monks and scribes.

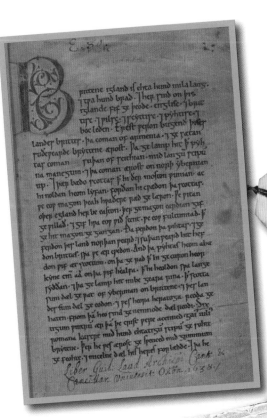

This is a page from the Anglo-Saxon Chronicle, which still survives today.

How do we know?

People sometimes unearth rare treasures with metal detectors. A man called Mr Baker, who had been metal detecting since the age of 10, made an unexpected find in a field 16 kilometres from Lincoln in 2002. Scraping away the soil, Mr Baker uncovered a rare 7th century sword hilt, belonging to a high-ranking Anglo-Saxon warrior. This was valued by the British Museum at over £100,000.

Finds like these are called 'treasure trove' and must be handed into a museum. Money for the treasure is shared between the person who has found the object and the owner of the land.

Most people in Lincolnshire lived in small villages at this time.

Dragons!

Villagers run for cover in the small Lincolnshire wood. Warriors have beached their dragon-headed boats by the mouth of the river and attacked the monks in the nearest monastery. They spared no one. Now they have set fire to a second monastery and, with their arms full of treasure from the church, they are making their way back to their boats. The villagers cower in the wood, praying to be saved from these ruthless Vikings.

Who were the Vikings?

The first known Viking raid on England was in AD 793. After this, more and more attacks hit the coasts of Britain. Raiders landed on the island of Lindisfarne, the Isle of Man, Ireland and Scotland. At first they came simply to steal food and treasure, particularly from monasteries and churches which had grown rich from the many gifts given to them. But, over the next two centuries, many Vikings settled in Britain.

The Vikings came from the countries we now call Norway, Sweden and Denmark. There had been a rapid growth in the population of this area and good farmland was scarce. So many groups of Vikings went overseas, seeking new places to find riches, or to settle.

Steer clear or I'll cut open your chest and spread out your ribs!

...AD 841 VIKINGS RAID LINCOLNSHIRE...AD 865 GREAT HEATHEN ARMY ARRIVES...

A Heathen Army

The first Viking raid on Lincolnshire took place in AD 841, with local monasteries and churches robbed of their riches. But worse was to come. In AD 865, the 'Great Heathen Army' arrived. This time the Viking warriors were determined to take over land. Soon all of eastern England fell under their control.

Under Viking rule, Lincoln became an important trading centre with connections to many parts of Europe. New timber buildings appeared and the town began to mint its own coins.

Divided Land

In AD 866, a large Viking army invaded East Anglia. It went on to conquer most of Northern England. Only one Anglo-Saxon kingdom held out against them. This was Wessex, in the west, whose ruler became known as Alfred the Great.

After a long struggle, Alfred defeated the Vikings in AD 886. They agreed to stay north of a line running from Chester to the Thames. This area was called the Danelaw. The Vikings founded many towns, including Derby, Leicester and Nottingham. They also built up trade links across the North Sea to mainland Europe.

This head was reconstructed from the skeleton of a Viking in the Great Heathen Army.

First the Vikings came to raid, then to trade, then they stayed.

How do we know?

Viking coins made in Lincoln are now part of the collection at Fitzwilliam Museum in Cambridge. Meanwhile, you can see the reconstructed Viking head at Derby Museum. Archaeologists have also discovered timber-framed buildings from Viking times in the Flaxengate area of Lincoln.

Rebellion

The Normans are building castles on land taken from the Saxons. The locals in Lincolnshire curse the new wooden and stone towers and ditches.

One man swears to avenge his father, who was brutally murdered by Normans for refusing to bow down to them. He has decided to join Hereward and his men in the fens. They are the only ones brave enough to fight!

I am one of William the Conqueror's men. William conquered all of England!

New arrivals

New invaders landed in Britain in 1066. These were the Normans from Northern France. Their leader, William, claimed that he had been promised the English throne. The Normans defeated the English army at Hastings, and William was crowned king. He established a strong government, headed by Norman noblemen.

Over the next 400 years, Britain changed from a collection of small kingdoms into just two independent nations. Soon after the Normans took control of all England, they also became overlords of Ireland. In 1282, English armies conquered Wales. Only Scotland remained free from English rule, after defeating them at Bannockburn in 1314.

SPOT THIS!

Some of the stained glass in this window at Lincoln Cathedral is over 700 years old.

TUDOR 1485–1603	STUART 1603–1714	GEORGIAN 1714–1837	VICTORIAN 1837–1901	MODERN TIMES 1901–NOW

Hereward the Wake

Hereward was an Anglo-Saxon nobleman from Bourne in south Lincolnshire. He hated the Normans for taking lands from his people. In the 1070s he led a rebellion, hiding out in the marshy fens of south Lincolnshire, with a base camp at the Isle of Ely. He earned the nickname 'Wake' which means 'watcher', as he spied out where best to attack the Normans. Hereward's hideout, however, was betrayed, and William attacked and killed most of the rebels. Hereward managed to escape and was never caught.

We don't know what Hereward looked like but many people saw him as a hero, as in this Victorian engraving.

People enjoyed throwing rotten food at criminals locked in the local pillory.

Ewww – rotten eggs! Being a medieval criminal really stinks!

How do we know?

After William had conquered England, he wanted to know what his new kingdom was worth. He sent out his men to gather the information, which was written down in the 'Domesday Book'. This huge document was completed in 1086 and gives us a good picture of what England was like at the time.

The Domesday Book also shows us that, within a few years, most of the Anglo-Saxon land had been given to Normans. We know that Hereward, for example, originally owned land around Crowland.

The Domesday Book is kept in the National Archives in London. In 2006, images of pages from the Domesday Book became available online.

Faith and Fear

Recently, people have been protesting against the changes that King Henry VIII has brought to the churches. At first there were many people who joined the march in Louth but as the days passed, the crowds melted away. They began to be afraid of what the king might do to them. No one stands in the king's way and those he considers as his enemies are quickly sent to their deaths.

The Tudor King, Henry VIII, made himself head of the church in England.

The Tudors

In 1485, the nobles of Lancaster won the Battle of Bosworth, which ended the Wars of the Roses. This brought a new family to the throne of England – the Tudors. They ruled for more than a century, until 1603, during which time huge changes took place in Britain.

The Tudor monarchs were strong and ruthless rulers. Henry VII made the country wealthy and peaceful again after a long civil war. Henry VIII broke England's links with the Roman Catholic Church, and opened the way for the Reformation. And Elizabeth I was a tough and inspiring leader, who survived plots against her life, and threats of invasion from France and Spain.

Changing Faith

Many people in Lincolnshire were angry at the changes Henry VIII made to the Church. An uprising began at Louth on 2nd October, 1536, and quickly spread to Horncastle, Caistor and Market Rasen. On 6th October, the protesters streamed into Lincoln from the surrounding countryside.

Henry VIII was furious and sent an army of 3,000 soldiers to put down the rebellion. Despite the large number of rebels (around 40,000), the protest fizzled out on 13th October.

Following the rising, the vicar of Louth and Captain Cobbler, two of the main leaders, were captured and hanged at Tyburn in London. Most of the other local ringleaders met the same fate, with a lawyer from Willingham being hanged, drawn and quartered for his part in the protest.

SPOT THIS!

Look out for deer in the grounds of Burghley House. There has been a deer park there since Tudor times.

FUN FACT

The great scientist Sir Isaac Newton discovered gravity while he was at home at Woolsthorpe Manor in Lincolnshire.

Protestors at Louth might have carried banners like this one, from the Pilgrimage of Grace march.

Peace and Poetry

The Tudor Age was a dazzling time for Britain. There was a long period of peace at home, while many other parts of Europe were torn by religious wars. This helped the country to become richer. The population grew, and so did farming and other industries. British seamen opened up new trading routes and founded colonies overseas.

The century also produced some of Britain's greatest writers, artists and composers. Greatest of them all was William Shakespeare, whose plays are still performed all over the world. Francis Bacon was one of the founders of modern science.

There is great excitement in the town. A troupe of players is setting up props in the local tavern and is about to perform one of the latest plays from London. The imaginary account on the right is written by a young boy whose father is mayor of Lincoln.

The play was written by a young man called William Shakespeare...

It was a day I shall never forget. We were invited as special guests to the performance of the Lord Chamberlain Players, who are making a rare visit outside London. Some people said they had come here to escape the plague!

The actors went to and fro, setting up scenery for a historical play called Henry V. When a trumpet sounded, the play began...

Henry V came onto the stage first and everyone cheered, for he had won great victories over the French. Meanwhile, fruit and food sellers worked their way through the crowds selling their goodies. But when it was time for the French princess to appear, I got quite a shock. It wasn't a woman at all but a young boy who played the part!

FUN FACT

Lincoln Cathedral was once one of the tallest buildings in the UK. But, in 1549, the spire on top of the tower blew off and was never replaced!

This reconstruction shows how Tupholme Abbey might have looked before it was destroyed.

Tupholme Abbey was closed by Henry VIII and was gradually demolished. These are the ruins you can see today.

Tudor kings and queens toured the country, staying at inns and manor houses.

How do we know?

The British Museum has a wax impression of the Tupholme Abbey seal, used to sign documents. The building itself, however, fell into ruin. In 1988, volunteers who wanted to preserve the site of the Abbey managed to rescue it. The Heritage Trust of Lincolnshire took over the Abbey's remains and opened the grounds to the public.

A computer reconstruction of the abbey was produced by bringing together evidence from a number of sources. Evidence included the standing remains of the abbey and its archaeology, aerial photographs and the remaining loose abbey stones.

New Machines

Farm workers in Lincolnshire are panicking. Farmer Jacob has brought in a new threshing machine that can do the work of ten men. The farm workers believe this will be the end of them – they'll be out of work and will starve. They will have to join the hunger queues. Something must be done. They decide to take drastic action: they will destroy the machines!

George III – or 'Farmer George' – was interested in farming and sometimes even dressed as a farmer!

Industrial Britain

The 19th century saw the peak of the industrial revolution in Britain. People from the countryside flocked to the new manufacturing towns to take jobs in mills and factories. Hours were long and wages were low, so that young children often had to work as well as their parents. Living conditions were also poor, with little clean water or sanitation, and many died of disease.

Slowly, things began to improve. New laws reduced the number of hours that women and children could work. Inspectors were appointed to check the safety standards of factories and mines. Wages were increased and, in 1871, the first bank holidays were introduced.

Food, Glorious Food

The population in Lincolnshire doubled between 1801 and 1851. This meant more people needed feeding. New farming methods and machinery were introduced and more land became farmland. In Lincolnshire this meant draining large areas of the fens.

The introduction of farm machinery met with riots in some areas as it was feared jobs would be lost. Around 1830, new machines were destroyed by gangs of farm workers in what were called the Swing Riots.

Lincolnshire, however, remained an important county for farming. Most Lincolnshire market towns were linked by rivers or newly built canals to carry grain to market. In the 1840s, railways were built so that goods could be transported even faster.

The Victorians

By late Georgian times, the British royal family had become very unpopular. People thought their rulers were weak and corrupt. Then in 1837, Victoria became queen, at only 18 years old. She reigned for over 60 years and restored respect for the monarchy.

During the Victorian Age, the British Empire grew to its greatest size. It covered nearly a quarter of the globe and included many millions of people. The Empire gave Britain vast supplies of valuable raw materials. It was also a huge market for selling British goods. Troops were stationed in most parts of the Empire, giving Britain a lot of power in the world.

Apart from the Swing Riots, this was a peaceful time for Lincolnshire.

FUN FACT
The first tomatoes grown in the UK were raised in the conservatory of Burghley House. At first people thought they were poisonous!

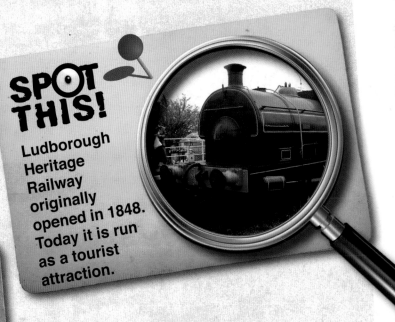

SPOT THIS!

Ludborough Heritage Railway originally opened in 1848. Today it is run as a tourist attraction.

Many people were desperately poor in Victorian times despite the wealth all around them. If families had nothing left, they could enter the workhouse.

I'm not looking forward to going to the workhouse. But it's our only choice.

Father tells us that there is nothing else left for us to do. After mother died, Father was injured at work. We have no money and must enter the workhouse. We are going there tomorrow.

Father tells us we must be brave. We will be separated from one another. Father will be in one part of the workhouse, me and my brothers in another and my sisters in yet another.

The food is not very good but at least we will be fed. We will also be put to work, usually doing boring work, such as picking tar from ropes so they can be re-spun.

It is very strict in the workhouse. If the rules are broken – and there are many rules, often for very small things – the punishments are severe. It is more like a prison than a place for helping the poor!

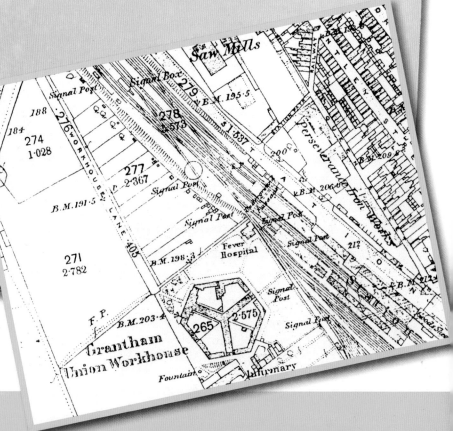

This map shows Grantham Workhouse in 1885, including an infirmary and a fever hospital.

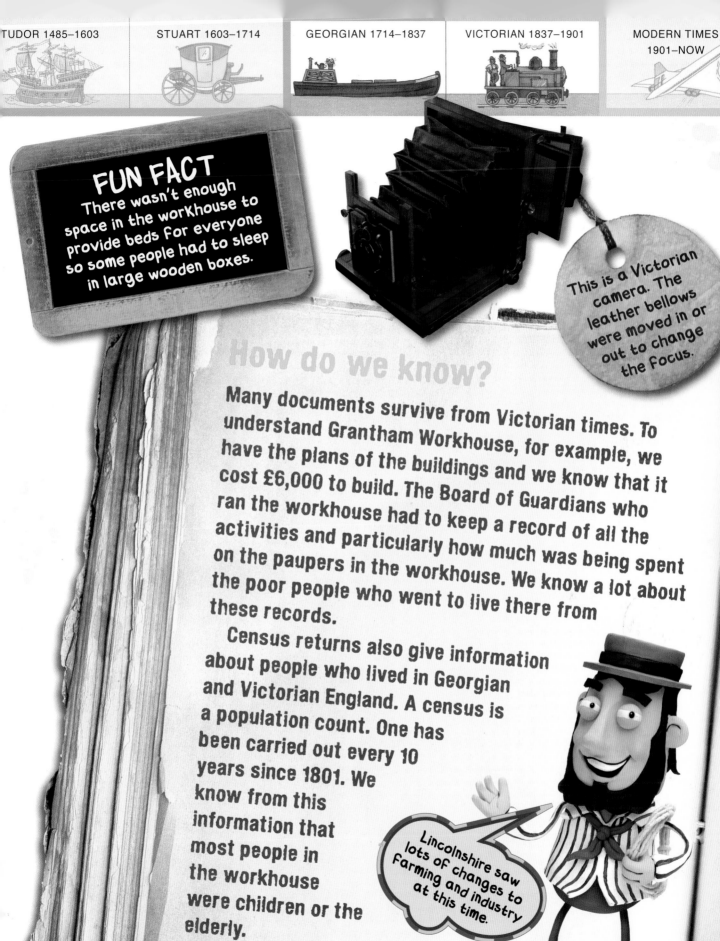

FUN FACT
There wasn't enough space in the workhouse to provide beds for everyone so some people had to sleep in large wooden boxes.

This is a Victorian camera. The leather bellows were moved in or out to change the focus.

How do we know?

Many documents survive from Victorian times. To understand Grantham Workhouse, for example, we have the plans of the buildings and we know that it cost £6,000 to build. The Board of Guardians who ran the workhouse had to keep a record of all the activities and particularly how much was being spent on the paupers in the workhouse. We know a lot about the poor people who went to live there from these records.

Census returns also give information about people who lived in Georgian and Victorian England. A census is a population count. One has been carried out every 10 years since 1801. We know from this information that most people in the workhouse were children or the elderly.

Lincolnshire saw lots of changes to farming and industry at this time.

23

Wartime

Grimsby is not safe. Since Britain has been at war, the town has been bombed. Bill and Susie are being evacuated to stay with their uncle and aunt, who live out in the countryside. They should feel lucky that they are staying with family – lots of other children will have to go and live with strangers. But neither Bill nor Susie wanted to leave their home.

Two World Wars

When Queen Victoria died in 1901, Britain was one of the world's richest and most powerful nations, with a massive empire and strong armed forces. But soon Britain was plunged into long and costly world wars. In World War One (1914–1918), around one million Brits were killed. Lincolnshire served an important part, with 37 airfields in use. Unfortunately they were too few to stop the Zeppelin air-ship raids on Cleethorpes in 1916.

World War Two (1939–1945) killed a vast number of civilians as well as soldiers. Enemy bombs destroyed large areas of major towns. The expense of the fighting left Britain with huge debts. The British Empire began to shrink as many countries demanded their freedom.

The Germans used Zeppelin airships to bomb Britain during World War One.

Bomber County

During World War Two, the Germans conquered most of Europe and were just across the North Sea, facing Lincolnshire. The county was in the front line again and airfields sprang up all over Lincolnshire, including at Digby, Wellingore, Coleby Grange and Hibaldstow. The RAF also had 29 bomber bases. There were so many airfields that the county earned the nickname 'bomber county'. The famous Dambuster Raid was launched from Lincolnshire and the jet engine was developed at RAF Cranwell.

Not long after World War Two ended, Britain and America fell out with Russia. Lincolnshire continued to be a location for bases of both British and American airforces. After 1989, Russia was no longer a threat and the bases were not needed.

SPOT THIS!

The casualty rate was very high among bomber pilots in World War Two. Can you spot the Wickenby RAF Memorial?

Hard Times

Britain took a long time to recover from the effects of World War Two. But by the 1960s the economy had grown strong again. In 1973, Britain joined the Common Market (now called the European Union), an organization which aimed to bring the countries of Europe closer together. In 1994, the Channel Tunnel was completed, linking Britain with mainland Europe.

There were also big changes in the way the British nations ruled themselves. In 1998, an agreement between the governments of Northern Ireland and the Irish Republic brought peace after 30 years of unrest and violence. In 1999, the people of Scotland and Wales voted to have their own parliaments and make many of their own laws.

Can you name Britain's First Female Prime Minister?

FUN FACT

Grantham gave us Britain's first policewoman, Edith Smith, as well as the first Female Prime Minister, Margaret Thatcher.

CELT 500 BC	ROMAN AD 43–410	ANGLO-SAXON AD 450–1066	VIKING AD 865–1066	MEDIEVAL TIMES 1066–148

As soon as war broke out in 1939, preparations were made to send children into the countryside where they would be safe from the bombs dropped on towns and cities. About 800,000 children were evacuated. This imaginary story is told by Alan, who is going to be sent from Grimsby to Bourne in Lincolnshire.

Grimsby is being bombed. At school we've done air-raid practice with our gas masks on. My best friend, Johnny, was sick in his. It made such a mess!

Last night, we were all asleep when the bombing started. We were sleeping downstairs under the big dinner table, as our air-raid shelter is not finished yet. The noise outside was like dustbins being kicked all over the place! I saw huge angry flames leaping from Gibson Street Church.

When the bombing stopped, we saw that the vibration of the bombs had brought all the cockroaches out of the ground. We all had our shoes in our hands, killing them.

The next day, all the kids were out looking in the street for pieces of burned metal from the bombs and bullet cases. Meanwhile, barrage balloons were flying overhead.

Later, we were making mud pies in the bomb crater where a land mine had blown up. This is too much fun! I don't want to leave and live in the smelly old countryside!

Government Air Raid Warning in 1939:

When you hear the warning take cover at once. Remember that most of the injuries in an air raid are caused not by direct hits by bombs but by flying fragments of debris or by bits of shells.

War-time gas masks are still in good condition because there were no gas attacks.

MINISTRY OF FOOD
R.B.2 16
CB 722595
(CHILD'S)
1953-1954
RATION BOOK
SERIAL NO.
Surname
Address

MINISTRY OF FOOD
R.B.1 18
AU 684378
1953-1954
RATION BOOK
SERIAL NO.
Surname
Address
Initials
F.O. CODE No.
E.11
IF FOUND RETURN TO ANY FOOD OFFICE

Many people kept their ration books after the war, giving us plenty of evidence of how rationing worked.

A week's worth of food rations for one adult

one egg
meat costing 6p
100g bacon and ham
50g cheese
180 ml milk
225g sugar
50g jam
50g tea
88g of sweets or chocolate

How do we know?

Some fighter and bomber pilots from World War Two are still alive today, as well as many of the children who were evacuated. Their stories are often posted on the internet and there are many programmes on television in which they talk about their experiences.

The 20th century is particularly rich in a variety of sources about World War Two. Photographs, newsreel film, newspapers and posters give us evidence of what it was like during the war. There are also groups of people who re-enact scenes from World War Two. This helps to bring the period to life.

Does anyone in your family remember Lincolnshire during World War Two?

CELT
500 BC

ROMAN
AD 43–410

ANGLO-
SAXON
AD 450–
1066

VIKING
AD 865–
1066

MEDIE
TIME
1066–1

Today and Tomorrow

Agriculture is still very important to Lincolnshire, with over 90 per cent of the county devoted to farming. In recent years the county has also become an oil and gas producer. Gas is piped ashore from the North Sea at Theedlethorpe. Roads and rail links have improved. Grimsby, Scunthorpe and Immingham are linked to the magnificent Humber Bridge. Tourism is important too. Skegness, Cleethorpes and Mablethorpe still attract thousands of holiday makers.

There is plenty of history to explore in historic buildings such as Tattershall Castle, still standing after nearly 600 years.

You can feel proud to be from Lincolnshire!

The Collection in Lincolnshire is the county's museum and art gallery. It has an activity centre for children and often holds special events.

This is a photograph of my grandfather, Mathew Robson (back row, far left), who played for Lincoln City before World War One. Up the City!

TUDOR
1485–1603

STUART
1603–1714

GEORGIAN
1714–1837

VICTORIAN
1837–1901

MODERN
TIMES
1901–NOW

FUN FACT

People from Lincolnshire are known as 'Yellowbellies'. This nickname may have come from the yellow waistcoats worn by the local soldiers.

▲ The Lincolnshire Show celebrates the continuing importance of agriculture to the county.

◀ The Ports of Grimsby and Immingham are situated near the mouth of the Humber Estuary. They are ideal for shipping goods between the UK and Europe. This is Grimsby Dock Tower.

BUTLIN'S SKEGNESS
General View showing Heated Pool

▲ Indoor attractions at Butlins in Lincolnshire have been added to make up for the poor British climate!

How will they know?

How will future generations know about Lincolnshire? Computers and the internet have given us the opportunity to explore past and present Lincolnshire. Digital cameras, video cameras and satellite images have all helped us to do this. Not only can we see history being made but we can also keep a digital version of our own personal history on our computers.

Glossary

AD – a short way to write anno Domini, which is Latin and means 'in the year of Our Lord', i.e. after the birth of Christ.

Aerial photograph – a photograph taken from high up in the air.

Air raid – a type of attack using planes to drop bombs. Air raids occurred during World War Two when German planes bombed Britain. Air-raid sirens warned people that planes were coming.

Archaeologist – a person who studies the past by looking at the remains left by previous people and cultures.

Artefact – an object, often an archaeological one.

Census – an official count of the population of a country.

Christian – a person who believes Jesus Christ is the son of God and follows his teachings.

Civil war – a war where people in the same country fight each other.

Domesday Book – a record of who owned property, land and animals in England in the 11th century.

Evacuate – having to leave your home and live somewhere else for safety.

Fen – low-lying, flat marshland.

Fort or fortress – a large, strong building offering military support and protection.

Gas mask – a mask to prevent you from breathing poisonous gas.

Hadrian's Wall – a wall that the Roman Emperor Hadrian ordered to be built across Northern England to keep out the North British tribes. Some of the wall still survives today.

Latin – the language originally spoken in Ancient Rome.

Missionary – a religious person who goes to other countries to tell people about the Bible and help those in need.

Monastery – a place where monks live and worship.

Monk – a male member of a religious community that has rules of poverty, chastity and obedience.

Pauper – a person who is very poor and who has no money and no possessions.

Pillory – a wooden frame with holes for the head and hands, used to punish criminals.

Port – a place, next to land, where the water is deep enough for ships to stop and stay.

Quernstone – another name for a mill stone, a small circular stone used for grinding corn.

Ration book – a book recording how much food you were allowed every week. Ration books were used during World War Two when certain foods were scarce and had to be shared fairly.

Scribe – a person who made hand-written copies of books, before printing was invented.

Treaty – a binding agreement, often of friendship, between two or more countries.

Workhouse – where poor people lived and worked when they had nowhere else to go.

Index

Air raids, 26
Alfred the Great, 13
Anglo-Saxon Chronicle, the, 11

Bacon, Francis, 17
Bardney, 9
Battle of Bannockburn, 14
Battle of Bosworth, 16
Battle of Hastings, 14
Blaecca, 9, 10
Boudicca, 4, 5
British Museum, the, 7, 11, 19
Burghley House, 17, 21
Butlins, 29

Caistor, 17
Captain Cobbler, 17
Census, the, 23
Channel Tunnel, 25
Claudius, 4
Cleethorpes, 24, 28
Coleby Grange airfield, 25
Collection, The, 28
Common Market (European
    Union), 25
Corieltauvi, 5, 7
Crowland, 9, 15

Dambuster Raid, 25
Danelaw, 13
Derby Museum, 13
Digby airfield, 25
Dissolution of the Monasteries,
    16
Domesday Book, the, 15

Elizabeth I, 16
European Union (Common
    Market), 25

Fitzwilliam Museum, Cambridge,
    13

Flaxengate, 13

George III (Farmer George), 20
Grantham Workhouse, 22, 23
Great Heathen Army, 12, 13
Grimsby, 24, 28
Grimsby Dock Tower, 29
Grimsby Port, 29

Hadrian's Wall, 5
Henry VII, 16
Henry VIII, 16, 17, 19
Hereward, 14, 15
Hibaldstow, 9
Hibaldstow airfield, 25
Horkstow Hall, 7
Horkstow Roman Villa, 4
Horncastle, 17
Hull Museum, 7
Humber Bridge, 28
Humber Estuary, 29

Iceni tribe, 5
Immingham Port, 29
Industrial Revolution, 20
Isaac Newton, Sir, 17
Isle of Ely, 15

Lincoln Cathedral, 14, 18
Lincolnshire Show, the, 29
Lindisfarne, 12
Lindsey, 8, 9
Lord Chamberlain Players, 18
Louth Rebellion, 16, 17
Ludborough Heritage Railway,
    21

Mablethorpe, 28
Market Rasen, 17

National Archives, 15
Newport Arch, the, 5

Norman Invasion, 14

Paulinus, Saint, 9, 10
Pilgrimage of Grace, the, 17

RAF Cranwell, 25
Reformation, the, 16
River Witham, 9
Roman Fort of Lincoln, 5

Scunthorpe, 28
Shakespeare, William, 17, 18
Skegness, 28
Smith, Edith, 25
Spaldingas, the, 9
St Giles Church, Scartho, 9
Swing Riots, 20, 21

Tattershall Castle, 28
Thatcher, Margaret, 25
Theedlethorpe, 28
Toutatis, 5
Treasure Trove, 11
Tudors, the, 16
Tupholme Abbey, 18, 28
Tyburn, 17

Vicar of Louth, 17
Victoria, 21, 24
Viking Invasion, 12

Wars of the Roses, the, 16
Wellingore airfield, 25
Wickenby RAF Memorial, 25
William the Conqueror
    (William I), 14, 15
Woolsthorpe Manor, 17
Workhouse, the, 22, 23
World War One, 24
World War Two, 24, 25, 26, 27

Zeppelin airship raids, 24

Acknowledgements

The publishers would like to thank the following people and organizations
for their permission to reproduce material on the following pages:

Cover: Shutterstock, Lee Hayward/Wikipedia, Polly-Alida Farrington/Flickr, Terence Mendoza/Shutterstock, Swindon Museum; p1: Mark Whitley/Flickr; p4: David Wright/Flickr; p5: Richard Southwell/Flickr; p7: Fishbourne Museum, Chichester; p9: Tony Milne/Flickr; p11: Lindisfarne gospe public domain/Wiki; p13: Roger/Wikipedia; p14: Revd Gordon Plumb/Flickr; p15: Mary Evans Picture Library/Alamy; p17: Chris Humphries/Flickr, Wikipedia; p19: Polly-Alida Farrington/ Flickr, reconstruction created by Antiquus Reconstruction, reproduced with the permission of Heritage Lincolnshire; p21: Paul Stainthorp/Flickr; p22: Peter Higginbotham/workhouses.org.uk; p23: Swindon Museum; p24: GL Archive/Alamy; p25: Brian Mossemenear/Flickr; p26: York Museums Trust; p27: Shutterstock; p28: Caroline Ward/The Collection, Lincoln, Mark Whitley/Flickr; p29: Picture by Lisa Warrener for the Lincolnshire Agricultural Society, Steve Parrott/Flickr, Glen Fairweather/Flickr.

All other images copyright of Hometown World

Written by Neil Tonge and Andrew Langley
Designed by Sarah Allen
Edited by Gemma Cary
Local history consultant: Pearl Wheatley

Illustrated by Leo Brown, Kate Davies, Dynamo Ltd, Virginia Gray,
Peter Kent, John MacGregor, Leighton Noyes and Tim Sutcliffe

First published by HOMETOWN WORLD in 2012
Hometown World Ltd
7 Northumberland Buildings
Bath BA1 2JB

www.hometownworld.co.uk

Lincolnshire County Council			
04763598			
A & H	03-Aug-2012		
J942.53 JNF	£4.99		
3599127	1222968/0028		

CELT
500 BC

ROMAN
AD 43–410

ANGLO-SAXON
AD 450–1066

VIKING
AD 865–1066

MEDIEVAL TIMES
1066–1485